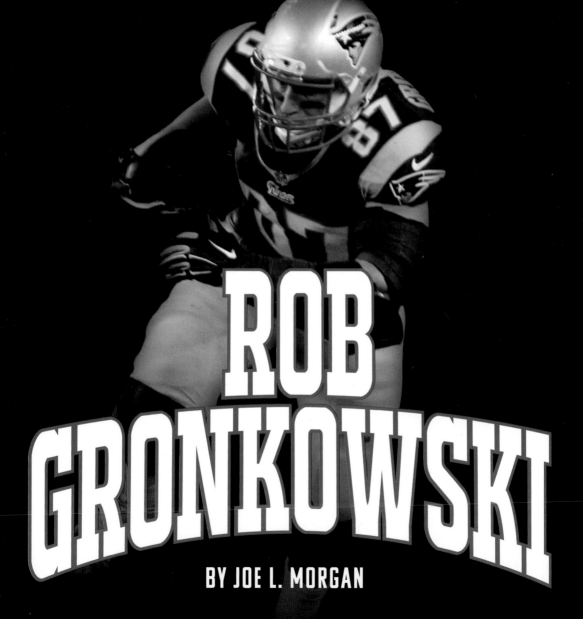

GRIDIRON GREATS
PRO FOOTBALL'S BEST PLAYERS

ROB GRONKOWSKI

BY JOE L. MORGAN

GRIDIRON GREATS
PRO FOOTBALL'S BEST PLAYERS

AARON RODGERS

ANTONIO BROWN

DREW BREES

J.J. WATT

JULIO JONES

ROB GRONKOWSKI

RUSSELL WILSON

TOM BRADY

VON MILLER

GRIDIRON GREATS
PRO FOOTBALL'S BEST PLAYERS

ROB GRONKOWSKI

BY JOE L. MORGAN

MASON CREST

Mason Crest
450 Parkway Drive, Suite D
Broomall, Pennsylvania 19008
(866) MCP-BOOK (toll-free)
www.masoncrest.com

First printing
9 8 7 6 5 4 3 2 1

ISBN (hardback) 978-1-4222-4074-8
ISBN (series) 978-1-4222-4067-0
ISBN (ebook) 978-1-4222-7725-6

Library of Congress Cataloging-in-Publication Data

Names: Morgan, Joe L., author.
Title: Rob Gronkowski / Joe L. Morgan.
Description: Broomall, Pennsylvania : Mason Crest, an imprint of National
  Highlights, Inc., [2018] | Series: Gridiron greats: Pro football's best
  players.
Identifiers: LCCN 2018020760 (print) | LCCN 2018022748 (ebook) | ISBN
  9781422277256 (eBook) | ISBN 9781422240748 (hardback) | ISBN 9781422240670
  (series)
Subjects: LCSH: Gronkowski, Rob, 1989—-Juvenile literature. | Tight ends
  (Football)—United States—Biography—Juvenile literature. | Football
  players—United States—Biography—Juvenile literature. | New England
  Patriots (Football team)—History—Juvenile literature.
Classification: LCC GV939.G777 (ebook) | LCC GV939.G777 M67 2018 (print) |
  DDC 796.332092 [B] —dc23
LC record available at https://lccn.loc.gov/2018020760

Developed and Produced by National Highlights Inc.
Editor: Andrew Luke
Interior and cover design: Jana Rade, impact studios
Production: Michelle Luke

CONTENTS

KEY ICONS TO LOOK FOR:

 Words to Understand: These words with their easy-to-understand definitions will increase the reader's understanding of the text while building vocabulary skills.

 Sidebars: This boxed material within the main text allows readers to build knowledge, gain insights, explore possibilities, and broaden their perspectives by weaving together additional information to provide realistic and holistic perspectives.

 Educational Videos: Readers can view videos by scanning our QR codes, providing them with additional educational content to supplement the text. Examples include news coverage, moments in history, speeches, iconic sports moments and much more!

 Text-Dependent Questions: These questions send the reader back to the text for more careful attention to the evidence presented there.

 Research Projects: Readers are pointed toward areas of further inquiry connected to each chapter. Suggestions are provided for projects that encourage deeper research and analysis.

 Series Glossary of Key Terms: This back-of-the book glossary contains terminology used throughout this series. Words found here increase the reader's ability to read and comprehend higher-level books and articles in this field.

WORDS TO UNDERSTAND

ACROBATIC – performing, involving, or adept at spectacular athletic feats requiring skillful control of the body

FOE – an opponent in a game or contest; adversary

TIGHT END – a pass eligible position in an American football offense

CHAPTER 1

GREATEST MOMENTS

ROB GRONKOWSKI'S NFL CAREER

Rob Gronkowski (commonly referred to by his nickname, Gronk), born May 14, 1989, is a former collegiate All-American and the NFL record holder for touchdowns made by a rookie **tight end**. He caught 90 passes for 1,327 yards in his second year in the league, is a three-time NFL All-Pro, and is a two-time Super Bowl champion. 2017 was Gronkowski's eighth year in the league, all with the New England Patriots as one of the most prolific tight ends to have played in the National Football League. He is in the company of such players as Kellen Winslow, Tony Gonzalez, and the great Mike Ditka.

The numbers that Gronkowski has put up in his career have been nothing short of amazing. His numbers for the 88 games he played through the 2016 season are on par with those of these players: Todd Christensen (1979–1985/NY Giants and Oakland); Vernon Davis (2006–2011/San Francisco); Jimmy Graham (2010–2015/ New Orleans and Seattle) and Kellen Winslow (1979–1986/San Diego).

Gronkowski has become a favorite target of future Hall of Fame quarterback Tom Brady. Through the end of the 2017 season, he has 405 receptions for 6,095 yards, and 69 touchdown catches. He is a member of four AFC Championship teams (2011, 2014, 2016 and 2017) and two Super Bowl Championship teams (XLIX and LI); he is also on pace to becoming enshrined in Canton, OH, as one of the best to play the position.

ROB GRONKOWSKI'S CAREER HIGHLIGHTS

In his first eight seasons Gronkowski has accomplished the following feats playing tight end for the New England Patriots:

- Set the single season NFL record for tight ends in 2011 with 1,327 receiving yards and 18 touchdowns.
- First tight end to lead the NFL in scoring with 108 points in 2011.
- Most double-digit touchdowns as a tight end in an NFL season: 2010 (10 touchdowns); 2011 (18 touchdowns); 2012 (11 touchdowns); 2014 (12 touchdowns); and, 2015 (11 touchdowns).
- Appeared in three of four Super Bowls as a member of the New England Patriots: Super Bowl XLVI (a February 5, 2012, loss to the New York Giants, 21-17); Super Bowl XLIX (a February 1, 2015, win over the defending Super Bowl champion
- Seattle Seahawks, 28–24); and Super Bowl LII (a February 4, 2018, loss to the Philadelphia Eagles, 41-33). Gronkowski did not play in the Patriots 34–28 overtime Super Bowl victory over the Atlanta Falcons on February 5, 2017, due to injury.
- Appeared in five NFL Pro Bowls (2011, 2012, 2014, 2015 and 2017).
- Named to four NFL First Team All-Pro teams (2011, 2014, 2015 and 2017).

GRONKOWSKI'S GREATEST CAREER MOMENTS

HERE IS A LIST OF SOME OF THE CAREER FIRSTS AND GREATEST ACHIEVEMENTS BY ROB GRONKOWSKI DURING HIS TIME IN THE NFL.

FIRST RECEIVING TOUCHDOWN

Gronkowski made his first NFL reception in his first game against the Cincinnati Bengals on September 12, 2010. The result? A 1-yard touchdown catch to increase the Patriots lead to 37–17, on the way to an eventual 38–24 victory.

Gronkowski receiving a 1-yard touchdown pass from quarterback Tom Brady in a September 12, 2010, game against the Cincinnati Bengals, his first game and touchdown catch as a pro.

FIRST 100-YARD RECEIVING GAME

Gronkowski finished his first professional season by recording the first 100-yard reception game in his career. He caught six passes for a total of 102 receiving yards and a touchdown, as the Patriots defeated division foe Miami by the score of 38–7, completing a 14–2 season.

In the final regular season game of his first professional season on January 2, 2011, Gronkowski had 6 receptions for 102 yards and one touchdown in a 38–7 win over division rivals, the Miami Dolphins, including this 13-yard, 1st-quarter touchdown catch for the game's first score.

FIRST MULTIPLE TOUCHDOWN GAME

Three of Gronkowski's 5 receptions and 53 of his 72 yards in a November 14, 2010, game against the Pittsburgh Steelers resulted in touchdowns from Tom Brady, the first time in his career that he scored multiple touchdowns in a game.

Gronkowski catches three touchdown passes of 9, 19, and 25 yards to help the Patriots fend off the Pittsburgh Steelers in a game on November 14, 2010.

FIRST 1,000-YARD RECEIVING SEASON

Rob Gronkowski improved upon his stats from his first NFL season by following up with a record-setting 1,327 receiving yards in year two. He became the first tight end in NFL history to lead all pass receivers (wide receivers, tight ends and running backs) in yards for a season.

In his second professional season, Rob Gronkowski finished the year with 1,327 receiving yards to lead all tight ends in the NFL. Here is Gronkowski on a 17-yard touchdown play as part of his 8-reception, 108-yard performance in a 49–21 victory over the Buffalo Bills on January 1, 2012.

FIRST 100-YARD RECEIVING PLAYOFF GAME

Gronkowski was on the Patriots team that lost to the New York Giants in the 2012 Super Bowl. On the way to the Super Bowl, he notched his first game with 100 or more yards receiving in the playoffs. Facing the Denver Broncos on January 14, 2012, Gronkowski caught the ball 10 times for 145 yards in a 45–10 victory in the AFC divisional round.

Gronkowski appeared in his second divisional playoff game and caught 10 passes for 145 yards, (an average of 14.5 yards per catch) in a January 14, 2012, win against the Denver Broncos. Here is one of his 10 catches, a 19-yard touchdown grab in the second quarter.

FIRST MULTIPLE TOUCHDOWNS IN A PLAYOFF GAME

Gronkowski made touchdown plays of 10, 12, and 19 yards in a divisional matchup against the Denver Broncos on January 14, 2012, the first time in his professional career that he caught the ball for multiple touchdowns in a playoff game.

While posting 145 yards receiving in a 45–10 win over the Denver Broncos in a January 14, 2012, game, Gronkowski also caught three touchdown passes, his first multiple-touchdown game in the playoffs. Gronkowski makes an **acrobatic** play in the end zone on this 10-yard touchdown play, which was upheld upon further review.

FIRST TIGHT END TO LEAD THE LEAGUE IN TOUCHDOWNS (2011)

2011 turned out to be a memorable season for Gronkowski. Not only did he lead the league in receiving yards and participate in his first Super Bowl game, he also led the league in touchdown catches with 18 for the season.

Gronkowski scores one of 2 touchdowns against Buffalo, January 1, 2012, on his way to becoming the first tight end in NFL history to lead the league in touchdown receptions.

FIFTH NFL PLAYER TO 50 TOUCHDOWNS IN FIVE SEASONS

During a 43–21 blowout victory over the Denver Broncos on November 2, 2014, Rob Gronkowski caught a 1-yard touchdown pass from Tom Brady in the 4th quarter. This touchdown reception resulted in Gronkowski's 50th TD in five years, making him one of five players ever to accomplish this feat in NFL history.

Gronkowski caught a 1-yard touchdown pass from Tom Brady against the Denver Broncos on November 2, 2014, for his 50th touchdown reception in five years.

Gronkowski played his first Super Bowl at Indianapolis in Super Bowl XLVI against the New York Giants.

TEXT-DEPENDENT QUESTIONS:

1. In which season did Rob Gronkowski lead all NFL tight ends in receiving? How many yards did he record for that year?
2. How many total receiving yards (through the 2016 season) does Rob Gronkowski have?
3. Against what team did Rob Gronkowski catch his first NFL touchdown pass?

RESEARCH PROJECT:

Gronkowski joined a list of only five players in NFL history to catch 50 touchdown passes in their first five seasons in the NFL (in his fifty-ninth game as a pro against the Denver Broncos on November 2, 2014). Make a list of the other four players and compare their statistics when they made their 50th touchdown reception. Determine who was the youngest, who was the oldest, who did it in the least amount of games, and who accomplished this task in the most games within five years.

The way Gronkowski's career is going, he may one day be on par with Hall of Fame tight ends like Kellen Winslow.

WORDS TO UNDERSTAND

CHRONIC TRAUMATIC ENCEPHALOPATHY (CTE) – a disorder of the brain that is caused by excessive concussions and other types of trauma or impacts to the head; athletes who participate in contact sports like football and boxing are at a greater risk of experiencing CTE than athletes who participate in other types of sporting events

FREE AGENT – a player who is not currently signed with or playing for a team

TANDEM – working together or as a pair

TRAGIC – an event that causes extreme emotional loss or is terribly painful by its nature

CHAPTER 2

THE ROAD TO THE TOP

Gronkowski was destined to become a great NFL star, based on the nature of his highly athletic family. Gronkowski is one of five brothers, three of whom played in the NFL (Chris, Dan, and Glenn) and an older brother (Gordie, Jr.) who played six seasons of minor league baseball. Having to compete in a family of professional athletes has made Gronkowski well suited to handling playing in the NFL for arguably one of the greatest franchises in NFL history, the New England Patriots. The Patriots took Gronkowski with the 42nd overall pick in the 2010 draft.

Here is a summary of the nineteen other tight ends selected in the 2010 draft and how they performed in the NFL:

Jermaine Gresham – Jermaine Gresham was the first tight end selected in the 2010 NFL Draft. He was selected 21st overall by Cincinnati Bengals out of the University of Oklahoma. He has made multiple Pro Bowl appearances as a tight end and has played for the Arizona Cardinals since the 2015 season.

Ed Dickson – The Baltimore Ravens drafted Dickson in the 3rd round out of the

University of Oregon. He not only appeared on Baltimore's Super Bowl XLVII championship team, but also played for the 15–1 Carolina Panthers team that lost to the Denver Broncos in 2015's Super Bowl 50. He signed with Seattle following the 2017 season.

Tony Moeaki – Moeaki played for several NFL teams in his career including Kansas City (which drafted him 93rd overall in the 3rd round), Seattle, and Atlanta. He has 91 catches for his NFL career, along with 1,201 receiving yards and 6 touchdowns, but has not played in the league since 2015.

Jimmy Graham – Graham was a 3rd-round pick of the New Orleans Saints'—the draft's 95th pick. A solid performer whose career has rivaled that of Gronkowski, he has more receiving yards and receptions than Gronk over the same seven-year period. Graham appeared in one Super Bowl while he was a member of the Saints and has played in five Pro Bowls; he has been named First Team All-Pro once. He is a current member of the Seattle Seahawks.

RESEARCH PROJECT

The Gronkowski brothers are a rarity in professional sports. Rob Gronkowski, along with his brothers Chris and Dan, all played in the NFL, and all for the same team. Rob and Dan played briefly together for the Patriots in 2011, while younger brother Glenn joined older brother Rob in the league in 2016. Brother Chris, between Rob and Dan in age, dressed for thirty-five games in the league over three seasons as a FB. Perform a little research to determine how many times brothers have played at the same time in the league (hint: look sharpe), and compare and contrast their results.

Gronkowski's teammate Aaron Hernandez was taken at TE in the same draft as Gronk, seventy-one picks later. The two were a formidable tandem until Hernandez's arrest ended his career.

Anthony McCoy, seen here at a practice for the 2010 Senior Bowl in his last season with University of Southern California, was drafted in the 6th round by Seattle.

Aaron Hernandez – Hernandez was a truly **tragic** case from the 2010 NFL Draft. Selected by the New England Patriots with the 113th pick in the 4th round from the University of Florida, Hernandez played the position in **tandem** with Gronkowski. During his NFL career, Hernandez caught 175 balls for 1,956 yards and 18 touchdowns. A conviction for first-degree murder of a friend resulted in his exit from the league. While serving time for that and another conviction (that was overturned on appeal), Hernandez was found dead in his jail cell at the age of twenty-seven on April 19, 2017. He was later diagnosed with severe **chronic traumatic encephalopathy (CTE)**, a disease that affects the brain of athletes who play contact sports.

Dennis Pitta – Pitta played college football at Brigham Young University and was drafted in the 4th round with the 114th pick by the Baltimore Ravens. He was a member of the Super Bowl XLVII championship Ravens team and has made 224 catches for 2,098 yards and 13 yards, averaging 9.37 yards per reception for his career, all with Baltimore. He retired before the 2017 season.

Garrett Graham – Graham was drafted by the Houston Texans from the University of Wisconsin at 118th in round 4 of the draft. During his time with the Texans, Graham made 100 catches for 1,059 yards and 10 touchdowns, for an average of 10.6 yards per catch and a touchdown per every 10 catches made. He has been out of the league since 2015.

Clay Harbor – Harbor was drafted by Philadelphia with the 125th overall pick in the 4th round of the 2010 NFL Draft. He also made stops in Jacksonville, New England, and Detroit, where he last played in 2016.

Michael Hoomanawanui – Hoomanawanui has eked out an NFL career as a 5th-round selection, drafted 132nd overall by the St. Louis Rams. He has 57 receptions and 646 yards for his NFL career as a tight end along with 8 touchdown receptions.

He also a member of the 2015 New England Super Bowl XLIX championship team and is now a member of the New Orleans Saints.

Andrew Quarless – Quarless was drafted to catch passes from Aaron Rodgers of the Green Bay Packers with the 154th pick in round 5 from Penn State University. Quarless was a member of the Packers Super Bowl XLV championship team in 2011. He signed as a **free agent** with Detroit in 2016, but a violation of league rules caused Quarless to be suspended for two games in 2016, and he was cut by the Lions; he is now out of the NFL.

Brody Eldridge – Eldridge was the 162nd pick and 5th-round selection of the Indianapolis Colts in 2010. He caught 14 passes and went for 84 yards in receiving in two seasons with the Colts. Drug problems have since derailed his career.

Fendi Onubun – Fendi Onubun was initially recruited out of high school to play basketball at the University of Arizona, where he did for four years under the legendary coach Lute Olson. Onubun transferred to the University of Houston, where he played an additional year as a tight end for the Cougars football team. It was his time at Houston that got him noticed by NFL scouts, where St. Louis spent their 6th-round selection to draft him 170th overall in 2010. Onubun played just four games with St. Louis and Jacksonville in a brief two-season NFL career.

Dennis Morris – Washington drafted Dennis Morris out of Louisiana Tech at pick 174 in the 6th round. He failed to make the team and is not currently in the NFL.

Nate Byham – Nate Byham was drafted by the San Francisco 49ers in the 2010 NFL Draft with pick number 182. He also spent time with the Tampa Bay Buccaneers during his short NFL career and made 11 catches for 83 yards and a single touchdown reception.

Anthony McCoy – McCoy was selected in round 6 by the Seahawks with the 185th pick in the draft. He spent time with Washington, and for his brief career, caught 31 passes for 437 yards and 3 touchdowns.

Mickey Shuler – Shuler, whose father (Mickey Shuler, Sr.) was an All-Pro tight end who played in the NFL for fourteen seasons from 1978–1991, was selected from Penn State University by the Minnesota Vikings with the 214th pick in the 7th round. Shuler's two receptions and 44 career receiving yards came as a member of the Vikings; he also was a member of Oakland Raiders, Jacksonville Jaguars, and Atlanta Falcons, before leaving the NFL altogether in 2015.

Dorin Dickerson – Dickerson was drafted 227th overall by the Seattle Seahawks in the 7th and final round of the 2010 draft. He played for three teams in just three seasons in the league with 11 career catches for 151 yards.

Check out this flashback of Rob Gronkowski's time in high school (2002–2005) showing his early skills at the tight end position.

Jim Dray – Dray was the draft's 233rd selection and was chosen by the Arizona Cardinals. Dray has 56 receptions and 605 yards with 3 touchdowns. He has also made stops in Cleveland, Buffalo, and San Francisco, rejoining Arizona for the 2017 NFL season.

Dedrick Epps – Epps was drafted by the San Diego Chargers in the 7th round and at pick 235; he was the last tight end drafted in 2010. With stops in both Miami and with the New York Jets, he caught just 1 pass for 9 yards in his six-game NFL career.

ATHLETIC ACCOMPLISHMENTS IN HIGH SCHOOL AND COLLEGE

Rob Gronkowski was born on May 14, 1989, in Williamsville, NY, a suburb of Buffalo. His parents, Gordon Gronkowski and Diane Walters, raised him and his four brothers in the nearby town of Amherst, NY, until he was seventeen, when the family relocated to Pittsburgh, PA.

HIGH SCHOOL

Gronkowski excelled at football both while playing in upstate New York and then in western Pennsylvania after the family moved. He caught the notice of many college recruiters and was a highly regarded tight end coming out of high school. He began his high school career in Amherst at Williamsville North High School (nicknamed the Spartans), playing his first three years before moving to play his senior year at Woodland Hills High School (nicknamed the Wolverines) located in Churchill, PA. As a junior, Gronkowski made 36 catches for almost 650 yards and caught 7 touchdowns. He also played on the defensive side of the ball as a junior and recorded 73 tackles, including 6 sacks on the quarterback.

GAMBLING ON GRONK

There was no doubting Gronkowski's physical ability as an NFL prospect. It was his ability to stay on the field that gave team's concern, and for good reason. Gronk entered the draft having missed his junior season recovering from surgery for a back injury. He had not played in about eighteen months. However, long-time New England head coach Bill Belichick liked Gronkowski's attitude and was convinced he was healthy after missing a season.

Belichick told reporters after picking Gronkowski, "I think you can see by the workout that he still has the same skills he had in 2008. I don't think that's a question and our doctors feel comfortable with his rehab and where he's at now. We go on their evaluations and recommendations. We have a deal. I don't diagnose the players and they don't call plays."

While in New York, Gronkowski made the All-Western New York first team and was an All-State second team honoree. He received the following honors after his senior year in Pittsburgh:

- All-American (SuperPrep and PrepStar)
- Associated Press (AP) Class 4-A All-State
- *Pittsburgh Post-Gazette* "Fabulous 22" honoree
- *Pittsburgh Post-Gazette,* First-Team All-Conference
- *Pittsburgh Tribune-Review* "Terrific 25"
- The *Harrisburg (PA) Patriot-News* "Platinum 33"

COLLEGE

After completing his senior year in high school as a member of the Woodland Hills football team, Gronkowski chose to play at the University of Arizona as a member of the Wildcat football team in the Pac-10 Conference. Gronkowski completed two full seasons with the Wildcats in 2007 and 2008. During his time as a member of the team, he accomplished the following:

- Freshman All-American (The Sporting News, Rivals.com – 2009)
- Freshman Pac-10, The Sporting News (2009)
- All-Pac-10 honorable mention (2009)
- John Mackey National Tight end of the week (twice – 2009)
- AP All-American (third team – 2008)
- All-Pac-10 (first team – 2008)

NFL DRAFT DAY 2010

Gronkowski entered the 2010 NFL Draft after sitting out his junior year in 2009 because of injury. His injury limited his participation in the 2010 NFL Scouting Combine, where he posted the following results:

- 40-yard dash: 4.61 seconds
- 3-cone: 7.18 seconds
- Vertical jump: 35.0 inches (0.89 m)
- Broad jump: 9 feet, 11 inches (3.02 m)

Gronkowski also participated in a pro day held at the University of Arizona. These were the results of his pro day experience:

Gronkowski was one of nineteen tight ends
selected at the 2010 NFL Draft in New York.

ROB GRONKOWSKI DRAFT DAY

The New England Patriots selected Rob Gronkowski in the draft's 2nd round with the 42nd overall pick.

NFL DRAFT DAY 2010
SIGNIFICANT ACCOUNTS

- The 2010 NFL Pro Draft was held at Radio City Music Hall in New York City April 22–24, 2010. It was the 75th pro draft held in the history of the NFL.

- Sam Bradford, quarterback, University of Oklahoma (Sooners) was the 1st overall pick in the draft, chosen by the St. Louis Rams.

- Bradford went on to win the Offensive Rookie of the Year Award for the 2010 season. Oddly enough, the 2nd pick in the draft, Nebraska DT Ndaamukong Suh, went on to win Defensive Rookie of the Year for Detroit.

- Cornerback was the most popular position drafted, with thirty-three players selected.

- The Philadelphia Eagles had the most selections, with thirteen in seven rounds. Philadelphia picked DE Brandon Graham from Michigan 13th overall with its first selection. Not a single one of those thirteen picks yielded a Pro Bowl-caliber player.

- The New York Jets had just four selections, the fewest in the draft, including 1st round pick Kyle Wilson of Boise State, taken 29th overall.

- The most successful draft was arguably that of the Seattle Seahawks, who chose four Pro Bowlers; 1st rounders OT Russell Okung (6th) and S Earl Thomas (14th), WR Golden Tate (60th), and S Kam Chancellor (133rd). All four played in Seattle's Super Bowl XLVIII win in the 2013 season.

- New England traded up two spots in the draft with Oakland to move ahead of Baltimore and take Gronkowski.

- Gronkowski and Jimmy Graham are the only draft picks from 2010 to be named NFL First Team All-Pros at TE.

- Measurements: 6 feet, 6.25 inches (1.99 m), 259 lbs (117 kg)
- 10-yard split: 1.58 seconds
- 20-yard split: 2.68 seconds

Gronkowski was expected to go somewhere in the middle of the 1st round in the 2010 NFL Draft but injury caused his stock to fall. Not taken until the 2nd round, he was the second tight end chosen in the draft out of twenty who were drafted that year.

GRONKOWSKI VERSUS THE 2010 NFL TIGHT END DRAFT CLASS

There were a total of twenty tight ends selected in the draft. Of the twenty drafted in 2010, only six have played long enough to record at least 100 catches. Here are the important statistics for each of those tight ends through 2017:

Round	#	Name	School	Team	REC	RecYDS	RecTD	Yrds/Rec
3	95	Jimmy Graham*	Miami (FL)	New Orleans	566	6800	69	12.2
2	42	Rob Gronkowski*	Arizona	New England	474	7179	76	15.1
1	21	Jermaine Gresham*	Oklahoma	Cincinnati	368	3658	29	9.9
4	114	Dennis Pitta	Brigham Young	Baltimore	224	2098	13	9.37
4	113	Aaron Hernandez	Florida	New England	175	1956	18	11.18
3	70	Ed Dickson*	Oregon	Baltimore	178	1985	12	11.2

*Active

TEXT-DEPENDENT QUESTIONS:

1. In which round was Rob Gronkowski selected in the 2010 NFL Draft? What was his overall draft number?

2. Who was the first tight end drafted in the 2010 NFL Draft? What college program did the first tight end draft selection play for?

3. How many tight ends were drafted in the 2010 NFL Draft? How many tight ends drafted in 2010 are still active in the NFL (as of the end of the 2017 NFL season)?

WORDS TO UNDERSTAND

INCEPTION – the beginning or start

FRANCHISE – an organization granted the right or license to operate as a member of a group or league

MUSTERED – brought into being

CHAPTER 3

ON THE FIELD

ROB GRONKOWSKI'S NFL ACCOMPLISHMENTS

One of the best players in NFL history to play tight end was Hall of Famer Raymond Berry, who played thirteen seasons for the Baltimore Colts of the AFL/NFL and led New England, as coach, to their first Super Bowl appearance in 1985. Here's a look at how the careers of Gronkowski and Berry compare:

Player	Years	REC	RecYDS	RecTD	Yrds/Rec
Raymond Berry	1955–1967	631	9,275	68	14.70
Rob Gronkowski	2010–present	474	7179	76	15.1

As you can see, Gronkowski's career totals are at or near the results **mustered** by Berry in his thirteen years with the Colts. This suggests that as long as Gronkowki stays healthy and continues to post the results that he has posted so far in his career, he is

Gronkowski's abilities on the field compare favorably to those of Hall of Fame TE Raymond Berry, a former New England Patriots head coach.

RESEARCH PROJECT

How good has Rob Gronkowski's NFL career been so far, compared to the greatest tight ends in the history of the league? What statistic best determines who is the best tight end? Pick a statistical category to determine how you want to compare the careers of different tight ends from each of these periods: the 1960s, 1970s, 1980s, 1990s, and 2000s. To make the comparison, you will need to pick a category, or set of categories to use for comparison (such as receptions, receiving yards, yards per reception, etc.). Once you determine which category to use, explain your reasoning for choosing it, and make a list of the top tight ends, one from each period above; see how Gronkowski compares to them based on your statistical reference point. Make sure your explanation takes each era and its style of play into account.

on pace to be as good if not better than one of the best to play the position in the NFL, the Hall-of-Famer Raymond Berry.

CAREER COMPARISONS

Here's how Gronkowski's career looks when compared to some of the best tight ends of all-time:

Player	Years	REC	RecYDS	RecTD	Yrds/Game
Tony Gonzalez	1997–2013	1,325	15,127	111	56.0
Jason Witten*	2003–2017	1,152	12,448	68	52.1
Antonio Gates*	2003–2017	927	11,508	114	52.3
Shannon Sharpe#	1990–2003	815	10,060	62	49.3
Ozzie Newsome#	1978–1990	662	7,980	47	40.3
Jackie Smith#	1963–1978	480	7,918	40	37.7
Greg Olsen*	2007–2017	639	7,556	53	45.8
Rob Gronkowski*	2010–2017	474	7,179	76	70.4
Vernon Davis*	2006–2017	548	7,072	60	39.3
Jimmy Graham*	2010–2017	556	6,800	69	56.2

* active
#Hall of Fame

GRIDIRON GREATS

ROB GRONKOWSKI
NEW ENGLAND PATRIOTS

TIGHT END

ROB GRONKOWSKI

Date of birth: May 14, 1989
Height: **6 feet, 6.25 inches (1.99 m),** Weight: **Approx. 223 lbs (101 kg)**
Drafted in the 4th round in 2010 (42nd pick overall) by the New England Patriots (the selection was the result of a trade with the Oakland Raiders)

CAREER

GAMES	RECEPTIONS	YARDS	AVERAGE	TD'S
102	474	7179	15.1	76

- Two-time Super Bowl champion (Super Bowls XLIX, LI). Gronkowski has totaled 8 catches for 95 yards in two appearances. New England lost Super Bowl XLVI to the New York Giants. Gronk was on injured reserve recovering from back surgery when New England won Super Bowl LI in 2017, but he did get a ring.
- Named first-team All-Pro four times (2011, 2012, 2014, 2015).
- Led the NFL in receiving touchdowns during the 2011 season with 17.
- Set NFL record for most touchdowns in a season by a tight end with 17 (2011).
- Set NFL record for most receiving yards in a season by a tight end with 1,327 (2011).
- Named the NFL Comeback Player of the Year for 2014 after missing nine games in 2013 with back and knee injuries.
- Selected as First-team All-Pac-10 (2008).
- Named Associated Press Freshman All-American (2007).

TIGHT END

RECORD-SETTING DAY

Gronkowski gave notice that he was a player to be watched on this day during his sophomore season at Arizona. In a Pac-10 Conference matchup against the University of Oregon Ducks on November 15, 2008, at Oregon's stadium in Eugene, OR, Gronkowski set the single-game record for receiving for Arizona tight ends. His 12-catch, 143-yard performance and one touchdown help fueled a second half comeback that fell just short as the Wildcats lost by the score of 55–45.

Highlights of Ron Gronkowski's performance against the Oregon Ducks on November 15, 2008, [go to the 2:10 mark for his touchdown catch against the Ducks].

The *Boston Globe* ranked many of the players at the tight end position who played for the New England Patriots since the **inception** of the **franchise** in 1960 (as the Boston Patriots). Here is a ranking of the top five tight ends by career receiving yards in New England's franchise history (of which Gronkowski would be on top):

Player	Years (w/Patriots)	REC	Rec Yards	TDs	Yds/Rec
Ben Coates	1991–1999	490	5471	50	11.17
Russ Francis	1975–1980; 1987–1988	207	3157	28	15.25
Jim Whalen	1965–1969	153	2487	17	16.25
Benjamin Watson	2004–2009	167	2102	20	12.59
Marv Cook	1989–1993	210	1843	11	8.78

Dallas TE Jason Witten is the active leader in catches and yards at the position through 2017, and second all-time. Gronkowski is on pace to match this career production, but would need to play and be healthy for another seven or eight seasons.

Coates, Francis, and Cook also appeared in ten Pro Bowls (Coates appeared in five) and were named First-team, All-Pro three times. Coates finished his NFL career with the Baltimore Ravens in 2000. He appeared in Super Bowl XXXV, catching 3 passes for 30 yards, while Francis, as a member of the San Francisco 49ers, was on the winning side in Super Bowl XIX against the Miami Dolphins, 38–16.

Here is another look at the top tight ends in New England history and their career stats (including all their NFL games) through the first 88 career games played, compared to Rob Gronkowski's NFL career results to-date:

Player	G	REC	Rec Yards	TDs	Yds/Rec
Rob Gronkowski	88	405	6095	68	15.05
Ben Coates	88	453	5071	48	11.19
Benjamin Watson	88	321	3776	28	11.76
Russ Francis	88	235	3431	32	14.60
Jim Whalen	88	197	3155	20	16.02
Marv Cook	88	225	2021	12	8.98

Gronkowski has already gained more receiving yards in 88 games than any other Patriot tight end did in his career. He has quickly established himself as one of the best to play the position of tight end, both as a member of the New England Patriots and in the history of the NFL. The longer he is able to play in the league, the more records he will smash as he places himself not only as the best tight end in the game, but as one of the best players in the game.

Russ Francis was a three-time Pro Bowl TE for New England in the mid-1970s, one of a handful of great players who have preceded Gronkowski at the position for the Patriots.

TEXT-DEPENDENT QUESTIONS:

1. Against what college opponent did Rob Gronkowski set the single-game record for receiving yards as a tight end for the University of Arizona?

2. Which Hall of Fame tight end coached New England to its first Super Bowl appearance?

3. Which team agreed to a trade with the New England Patriots to allow them to select Gronkowski with the 42nd pick overall in the 2010 NFL Draft?

WORDS TO UNDERSTAND

LITERARY – of or relating to books

OFF-THE-CUFF – not prepared in advance; spontaneous

ORATOR – one distinguished for skill and power as a public speaker

SARDONIC – characterized by bitter or scornful ridicule or mockery; cynical; sneering

CHAPTER 4

WORDS COUNT

When the time comes to address the media before or after a game, players either retreat to the comfort of traditional phrases that avoid controversy (Cliché City), or they speak their mind with refreshing candor (Quote Machine).

Here are ten quotes from Rob Gronkowski, compiled in part from the website 247Sports.com and the *Boston Globe*, offering some context to what he was referencing. As this list attests, Gronk is quite a character and may not know what a cliché is.

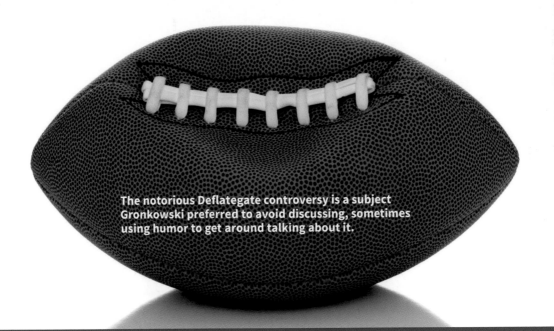

The notorious Deflategate controversy is a subject Gronkowski preferred to avoid discussing, sometimes using humor to get around talking about it.

"I only read, like, 80 percent of it. I know where all the parts are, though."

Rob Gronkowski wrote a book about his life in football called, *It's Good to Be Gronk,* a *New York Times* best seller co-written by Jason Rosenhaus. This quote is the response to being asked whether or not he actually read the book. His reply candidly indicates that although he did not read a significant portion of the **literary** work, he at least knows how it is organized and what the book says. **Rating: Quote Machine**

"You know, these sure aren't deflating. These are only inflating."

Gronk made this comment in reference to the infamous Deflategate controversy, in which the Patriot's superstar QB Tom Brady was suspended for illegally having game footballs partially deflated to make them easier to grip. This tongue-in-cheek response about his bicep muscles was meant to avoid comment on the issue by deflecting with humor. **Rating: Quote Machine**

Gronkowski dreamed of becoming a professional wrestler before choosing football.

"At one time, I wanted to be a WWE wrestler. I still do. I want to go in the ring once and mess around and jump off the ropes and do a Stone Cold stunt."

Gronkowski also played baseball and basketball while attending high school and has expressed an interest in exploring other types of sports competition, such as professional wrestling. This quote is in keeping with his youthful excitement toward life and feeling of invincibility as he discusses his desire to perform wrestling moves in the ring similar to pro wrestling star Steven "Stone Cold" Austin. **Rating: Quote Machine**

"**Best dancer? I mean, since I'm the only one who really whips out any dance moves, I'd have to go with myself.**"

When it comes to moves on the dance floor or in the end zone, there is no better dancer on the team than Rob Gronkowski. This is according to Rob Gronkowski, who gave this quote when asked his opinion on the subject. **Rating: Quote Machine**

"**When you block someone and put them on their back, that's called a pancake. Those are the best pancakes. Because I get hungry during games.**"

Gronkowski demonstrates his enthusiasm for the physical aspect of the sport with this quote, while remaining true to form in maintaining his humorous side. **Rating: Quote Machine**

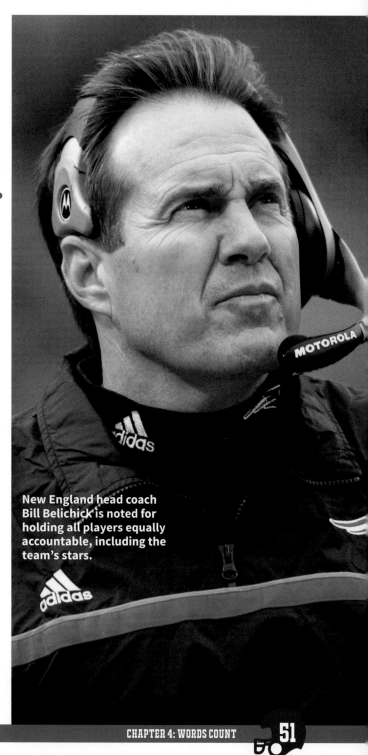

"He's murdered everyone before. I've been murdered before. Brady's been murdered. A new guy that goes out to practice and he was there for one day I seen get murdered before ."

Gronkowski colorfully discussed coach Bill Belihick's tendency to "murder"(read "yell at emphatically") any player who has it coming, from the star QB or TE to a player at his first practice. Gronk was making the point that Belichick holds all players equally accountable. **Rating: Quote Machine**

New England head coach Bill Belichick is noted for holding all players equally accountable, including the team's stars.

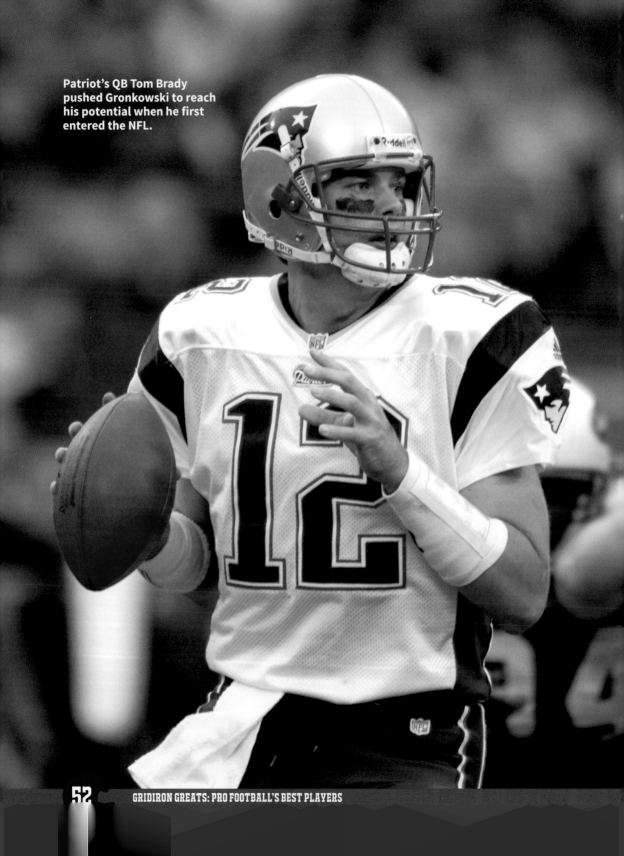

Patriot's QB Tom Brady pushed Gronkowski to reach his potential when he first entered the NFL.

> "[Brady] always used to yell at me and get on my case. I was like, 'Man, this dude, why is he coming at me like that?' He would always be making sure my routes were on point, yelling at me to be where I've gotta be. Then he came up to me one day and he was like, 'Yo, Rob, you know I love you. I just see a lot of potential in you.'"

Few people in the NFL doubt that quarterback Tom Brady will go down as one of the greatest if not the greatest quarterback ever to play professional football. Over his eighteen-year career, he has won five Super Bowl championships, been named to thirteen Pro Bowl games and named First Team All-Pro three times, in addition to the countless other awards and honors that he has received. When Gronkowski entered the league in 2010, he was a rookie who needed to distinguish himself as a pass catching tight end. Brady saw a talent level in Gronkowski and made it his mission in their first several years together to get Gronkowski to realize his potential greatness. **Rating: Quote Machine**

A Spanish-language reporter, when questioning Gronkowski's reported partying ways, was provided the quoted answer in Spanish, demonstrating the extent of Gronk's bilingual skills. **Rating: Quote Machine**

> "Yo soy fiesta (I am a party)."

NEXT QUESTION

Gronkowski, along with his father Gordon Sr. and brothers Dan, Chris, Glen, and Gordie Jr., were interviewed for a segment of the news program *CBS This Morning.* The interview took place during a time when the team was dealing with the shocking details of teammate and fellow tight end Aaron Hernandez's trial. Gronkowski, attempting to keep the interview about the family and away from the controversy surrounding the team and Hernandez, repeated the phrase "Next Question," which he said he learned from his agent, Drew Rosenhaus.

Watch this tense moment as the news show *CBS This Morning* tries to get Rob Gronkowski to open up about his teammate's (Aaron Hernandez) upcoming trial.

"I didn't see any replays or anything like that, but did you guys see any time where the ball hit the ground? [Reporters say 'No'] That's because it didn't. That's why. I put my hand underneath the ball. I know for sure I caught it and I just don't understand why it wasn't a TD."

Following a Week 10 41–16 win over Denver on November 12, 2017, Gronkowski strongly maintained that a play in which he was ruled to have not made a catch at the goal line was called incorrectly, despite the fact that it was upheld after replay challenge. **Rating: Quote Machine**

Dunkin Donuts, a national coffee maker and donut chain, is based in Boston and are huge supporters of the New England Patriots (and other local pro sports teams). The quote was an **off-the-cuff** remark from Gronkowski while being interviewed for a Thanksgiving video produced by the sponsor in which he shows off his cooking skills. When asked if he had cooking experience, Gronk explained that at college at Arizona, he would often cook for his friends in the wee hours of the morning. This quote reflects his assessment of how his cooking turned out on those occasions. **Rating: Quote Machine**

"Most tasty meals at 2:00 a.m., ever."

THE BILINGUAL GRONK

Rob Gronkowski may be talented as a pass receiver at the tight end position but he is not quite as equally skilled as a color analyst—especially broadcasting in German! The evidence of this disparity in talents surfaced in a video from November 7, 2016, as posted on the Twitter account of Sebastian Vollmer, an eight-year NFL offensive tackle who played for New England (alongside Gronkowski) known as the "Seabass." The Seabass was born in Kaarst, Germany, and was one of a handful of foreign players in the NFL. He tried to help Gronk with some simple German descriptions and sayings, with predictably hilarious results.

Sebastian "Seabass" Vollmer and Rob "Gronk" Gronkowski highlighting the Gronk's plays in German, as posted to Twitter, November 7, 2016.

QUOTE

Rob Gronkowski Acceptance Speech for the Ron Burton Community Service Award

Gronkowski is known for **sardonic** comments that inspire Internet memes; but he is not one who has been considered a great **orator** while a member of the New England Patriots. Gronkowski was the recipient of the Ron Burton Community Service Award in 2016 for his work in the Boston community. The award is named for Ron Burton, the 1st draft selection of the then expansion Boston Patriots in 1960 and recognizes the Boston-area athlete in any sport who has done the most in the community.

Past winners of the award include Boston College quarterback Doug Flutie, former Boston Celtics great JoJo White, and Kristine White, a member of the U.S. Women's National Soccer team. Although Gronkowski is not as well known for giving great speeches, here is an excerpt of the acceptance speech he was able to deliver for the award:

"This is an honor to accept this award. Who would ever have thought that five years ago when I was on ESPN every weekend [partying] that I would be accepting this award [laughs]. But...I just want to thank you Mr. Kraft on behalf of your family, the Burton family thank you so much, and this award will definitely be right in front of my trophy case. Thank you, guys."

Gronkowski certainly never misses an opportunity to tell a joke but his remarks were sincere in accepting the Ron Burton award in recognition of his work and the dedication to helping those in need in the community.

Gronkowski thanked Patriots' owner Robert Kraft when he received the Ron Burton Community Service Award in 2016.

RESEARCH PROJECT

Although Rob Gronkowski tends to be a straight shooter when speaking to the media and doesn't pull his punches when discussing certain things that should be off limits, he also tends to be private and reserved about certain personal issues, such as his family or dating. Who is more private, Rob Gronkowski or Tom Brady? To answer this question, take a look at news articles from the past five years (2013–2017) and keep a count of the number of times that either athletes provided a quote on a personal subject. Write an opinion, citing sources, about which of the two is more guarded with his personal issues.

A COMMITMENT TO HEALTHIER LIVING

Gronkowski has been injured many times in his career, resulting in many surgeries, which were responsible for him missing twenty-four of eighty-eight games played through the end of 2016, or a little more than one-quarter of those games. Marveling at health and longevity of his teammate and leader of the Patriots, forty-year-old Tom Brady, the twenty-seven-year-old Gronkowski was inspired to make some changes in his habits in order to experience some career longevity of his own and to stay on the field during NFL seasons.

As reported by the *Boston Herald* in August 2017, Gronkowski started a training program for the purpose of strengthening his body and staying healthy in order to play longer and make it through an entire season with fewer injuries, stress, and strain on his body. About his new dedication to fitness, Gronkowski said:

"I wanted to find a way to make me feel good all the time and not worry. I'm getting massage therapy, I'm learning about hydration, I'm learning about nutrition. It's helping me expand my game."

The new approach to training and fitness has also caught the attention of Brady, who has become one of Gronkowski's supporters and is helping him stay focused by occasionally preparing a plant-based meal for him as an example of something that helps him to stay healthy. When asked about Brady's involvement in helping him stay on track, Gronkowski was quoted as saying:

"Tom's my chef. I told him I'm only eating them (plant-based meals) if you have them ready for me. And he said, 'Deal.'"

One of the ways in which Brady and Gronkowski's trainer works with him is to plan for those inevitable occasions when Gronk strays from his healthy eating habits by drinking coffee and alcohol. Every time he goes off-plan and consumes alcohol and caffeine, he is required to drink three glasses of water. Gronkowski has, for the most part, stayed within the plan and has noticed the results: "I feel looser. I feel my mobility has increased a lot. I feel way more pliable."

A Rob Gronkowski who is healthier, focused, leaner, and meaner may result in great success for the New England Patriots and will continue to widen the gap between the team and the rest of the league when it comes to winning championships.

Gronkowski, seen here at Patriots training camp, has reflected on his training methods in recent years and vowed to improve them to help him stay healthy.

TEXT-DEPENDENT QUESTIONS:

1. What Boston-area food chain is a supportive sponsor of the Patriots?

2. What year was Rob Gronkowski the recipient of the Ron Burton Community Service Award for his work in the Boston community?

3. What is the title of the book Gronkowski co-authored with Jason Rosenhaus in 2015?

WORDS TO UNDERSTAND

AUTISM – a spectrum of pervasive developmental disorders of children, characterized by impaired communication, excessive rigidity, and emotional detachment

CELEBRITY – a person who is noted and famous

FOUNDATION – a charitable organization that distributes funding to other organizations in support of a stated mission or charitable purpose

PARKINSON'S DISEASE – a degenerative disease of the central nervous system that effects fine motor skills and causes tremors in sufferers

REARING – raising or bringing up a child to maturity

CHAPTER 5

OFF THE FIELD

LET'S PLAY THE FAMILY FEUD

Gronkowski, his father, Gordon Sr., and his brothers—Gordie Jr., Dan, and Chris—came together to play *Celebrity Family Feud*. The syndicated television game show matches **celebrity** families from different aspects of the entertainment field, like sports, movies, television, and other entertainment areas allowing them to compete for up to $25,000 for their favorite charity or cause. The Gronkowskis were pitted against the Peete family, featuring actress Holly Robinson-Peete and husband Rodney Peete, a former NFL quarterback (who finished second in the Heisman Trophy voting in 1988 to running back and future Hall of Fame inductee Barry Sanders).

The Peetes appeared on the show to raise money and awareness for their Hollyrod **Foundation**. The organization raises money for families either **rearing** children with **autism** or living with individuals with **Parkinson's disease**. Gronkowski's appearance on the program was in support of Rodman Ride for Kids, an annual event that raises money for at-risk children growing up in Massachusetts.

After speaking with the show's host comedian Steve Harvey about his popularity on YouTube with some of his dance moves, Gronkowski accepted a challenge from one of the audience members to show some of his dance steps. After impressing everyone with his dancing ability, he proceeded to face Holly Robinson-Peete as the respective heads of their family. The first challenge was "Name something that inflates and deflates," and Gronkowski pretended to be upset in refusing to participate in answering it. The question was a joke alluding to the Patriots' recent Deflategate scandal involving quarterback Tom Brady. The Peetes went on to win the contest over the Gronkowski clan in convincing fashion.

Gronkowski and his family faced former NFL QB Rodney Peete and his clan (seen here at a movie premier) on a sports celebrity version of the popular TV game show *Celebrity Family Feud.*

The entire clip from the episode of the *Celebrity Family Feud* featuring Rob Gronkowski and his family against Holly Robinson-Peete and her family.

GIVING BACK TO THE COMMUNITY

Gronkowski takes the time to give a lot back to the community. He is involved in many community-based efforts and is a great community ambassador for the team and himself, according to New England Patriots owner Robert Kraft, due to his easy going, happy-go-lucky approach to life. His work has included partnering with many local and national charitable organizations, schools, hospitals, and the military, such as:

- Make-A-Wish Foundation – A national organization that works on behalf of terminally ill children to provide them with opportunities to fulfill some life dream or goal.

- Massachusetts General Hospital and Boston Children's Hospital – For the Boston Children's Hospital, Gronkowski has participated in shaving his head to raise money and awareness toward childhood cancer. He has also involved himself in employee

Gronkowski has worked with the local chapter of the Make-A-Wish Foundation in Boston, an organization that grants wishes for terminally ill children.

and volunteer recognition programs at Massachusetts General Hospital.

- Department of Defense – Gronkowski is passionate in his support for those Americans serving in the military and the sacrifice made by military families.

- Play 60 – Play 60 is an effort by the NFL to promote physical activity, healthy lifestyles, and healthy eating for children. The name comes from the core concept of the program of getting children to be active for at least 60 minutes a day, getting them away from sedentary pursuits like watching television or using other electronics or mobile entertainment devices.

Gronk has also been involved with Celebrities for Charity and works to make himself available for as many opportunities to help children and youth less fortunate as he can. He was quoted in an ESPN.com article as saying, "I was always blessed growing up with opportunities and access to facilities, equipment, and playing with my brothers in the backyard to be the best athlete I could be. Everyone always helped me out growing up, and everyone now supports me on Sundays. So whenever there's a chance to give back, to the community, to the less fortunate kids so they have the opportunity to gain the most potential they can in their life to be a success, it's always good to do."

Taking underprivileged children to Foxborough, the home of the Patriots' Gillette Stadium, has been something that Gronkowski feels helps him connect with communities of all types and make the Patriots experience accessible to all of the youth in those communities, while helping to instill a love for the sport.

MARKETING ROB GRONKOWSKI

Gronkowski signed a six-year, $54.4 million contract extension with the New England Patriots in 2012 that kicked in for the 2014 season. The contract, the richest at the time for the tight end position, keeps Gronkowski with the team through the 2019 season, with $31.75 million in base salary and more than $22 million in bonuses and incentives for him to stay in a Patriot's uniform. The Patriots restructured the contract before the 2017 season to add the possibility of an additional $5.5 million a year in bonuses and incentives. Gronk has admitted, however, that most of the money he lives off of that allows him to be as active as he is does not come from his huge contract. His marketing activities give him more than enough to live on and enjoy life.

Gronkowski's rugged good looks and boy-next-door charm makes him a natural for advertisers and others looking to promote their products and services. Gronkowski has used his time in NFL to connect to younger consumers. His name and face are as recognizable, if not more so, than most players in the league who are not Brady, Aaron Rodgers (Green Bay Packers QB), or Cam Newton (Carolina Panthers QB).

Like Jet's QB Joe Namath did in his career in the 1970s, Gronkowski has realized that he should maximize his marketing opportunities while his career is in full bloom.

RESEARCH PROJECT

Rob Gronkowski signed a huge contract worth more than $54 million over six years that makes him one of the richest tight ends in the history of the NFL. The true bulk of his income, however, comes from his marketing activities. What other NFL players, currently in the league as of 2017, make a large part of their income from marketing activities? Research online and determine the top five NFL players who make at least $1 million or more in income related to promoting products and services. Who ranks first in the league? How much does each player earn annually in promotions, endorsements, and other marketing activities?

One of the ways that Gronkowski has been able to promote himself and stay relevant to younger audiences is through his Gronk's Party Ship vacation cruise. The vacation package provided die-hard fans of Gronkowski a way to come together and celebrate everything "Gronk," further solidifying his standing as king of the millennial bros.

Gronkowski's attitude toward promoting himself comes from a legendary example, Hall of Fame quarterback Joe Namath. Joe Namath realized early in his career that he needed to maximize all of his earning opportunities, promoting everything from men's personal care products to woman's pantyhose, which he did in a famous 1974 commercial for Hanes Beautymist Pantyhose. Gronkowski may not take to wearing women's pantyhose anytime soon, but you never know what opportunities he may choose.

ROB GRONKOWSKI'S BRAND MANAGEMENT

Gronkowski is represented by powerhouse sports agent Drew Rosenhaus, who represents more than 170 players. He has on his roster of clients such notable players as Pittsburgh Steeler receiver Antonio Brown, T.Y. Hilton of the Indianapolis Colts, and Steelers' cornerback Joe Haden.

With Rosenhaus, who is also an attorney and a graduate of Duke University's School of Law, representing his contract with the Patriots, Gronkowski has been busy getting his face on the cover of EA Sports Madden NFL 17 video game, a much sought-after honor for NFL players. Additionally, Gronk has made appearances on late night television shows, such as *Jimmy Kimmel Live*, and made guest appearances on several television shows as himself. He is also the executive producer of a show called *MVP*, a version of the popular ABC television show *Shark Tank*, where budding business owners and inventors present their ideas to a panel of athletes for funding. By attracting a high level of attention to himself, Gronkowski knows that he will be able to remain relevant to the public long after his football playing days are over.

A FAMILY AFFAIR

Gronkowski has been able to get his professional sports playing brothers into the act as well. The brothers have come together to form Gronk Nation. Gronk Nation provides an online store for the purchase of Gronkowski themed merchandise and other items for fans of Rob Gronkowski. Some of the proceeds that come from the sale of Gronkowski's merchandise goes toward funding for the Gronk Nation Youth Foundation, the charitable arm of Gronk Nation L.L.C. It is through Gronk Nation Youth Foundation that Gronkowski and his family have created partnerships with such companies as Boston-based John Hancock Financial and others to sponsor such events as the 2013 Boston Marathon and many community-based youth initiatives.

A bit of controversy arose between Gronk Nation and shoe company Nike, whose brand Gronkowski wears on the field. The logo used for Gronk Nation features an image of Gronkowski spiking a football, similar to his signature move when scoring a touchdown. The image, when examined closely, appears similar to the famous Jumpman logo that Nike has used in connection with its Air Jordan brand basketball shoes. The Jumpman logo features basketball superstar and NBA Hall of Famer Michael Jordan and is perhaps one of the most recognizable logos in sports. Nike filed a dispute with the U.S. Patent and Trademark Office for resolution.

Regardless of the outcome of the dispute, it is clear that Rob Gronkowski has been successful in banking on his career and turning his time in the NFL so far into an opportunity to benefit himself, his family, and the community that has supported him.

The two-time Super Bowl champion presented a $70,000 check to six New England school districts in May 2017 on behalf of his Gronk Nation Youth Foundation, which is dedicated to inspiring and supporting youth through sports.

TEXT-DEPENDENT QUESTIONS:

1. What is the name of the name of charity Rob Gronkowski supported in his appearance on Celebrity Family Feud?

2. What is the name of the organization that Gronkowski shaved his head for on behalf of children cancer patients?

3. What was the total value of the contract extension Gronkowski signed with the New England Patriots in 2012?

blitz – a defensive strategy in which one or more linebackers or defensive backs, in addition to the defensive line, attempt to overwhelm the quarterback's protection by attacking from unexpected locations or situations.

cornerbacks – the defenders primarily responsible for preventing the offenses wide receivers from catching passes, accomplished by remaining as close to the opponent as possible during pass routes. Cornerbacks are usually the fastest players on the defense.

defensive backs – a label applied to cornerbacks and safeties, or the secondary in general.

end zone – an area 10 yards deep at either end of the field bordered by the goal line and the boundaries.

field goal – an attempt to kick the ball through the uprights, worth three points. It is taken by a specialist called the place kicker. Distances are measured from the spot of the kick plus 10 yards for the depth of the end zone.

first down – the first play in a set of four downs, or when the offense succeeds in covering 10 yards in the four downs.

fumble – when a player loses possession of the ball before being tackled, normally by contact with an opponent. Either team may recover the ball. The ground cannot cause a fumble.

goal line – the line that divides the end zones from the rest of the field. A touchdown is awarded if the ball breaks the vertical plane of the goal line while in possession or if a receiver catches the ball in the end zone.

huddle – a gathering of the offense or defense to communicate the upcoming play decided by the coach.

interception – a pass caught by a defensive player instead of an offensive receiver. The ball may be returned in the other direction.

lateral – a pass or toss behind the originating player to a teammate as measured by the lines across the field. Although the offense may only make one forward pass per play, there is no limit to the number of laterals at any time.

line of scrimmage – an imaginary line, determined by the ball's location before each play, that extends across the field from sideline to sideline. Seven offensive players must be on the line of scrimmage, though the defense can set up in any formation. Forward passes cannot be thrown from beyond the line of scrimmage.

pass – when the ball is thrown to a receiver who is farther down the field. A team is limited to one such forward pass per play. Normally this is the duty of the quarterback, although technically any eligible receiver can pass the ball.

play action – a type of offensive play in which the quarterback pretends to hand the ball to a running back before passing the ball. The goal is to fool the secondary into weakening their pass coverage.

play clock – visible behind the end zone at either end of the stadium. Once a play is concluded, the offense has 40 seconds to snap the ball for the next play. The duration is reduced to 25 seconds for game-related stoppages such as penalties. Time is kept on the play clock. If the offense does not snap the ball before the play clock elapses, they incur a 5-yard penalty for delay of game.

punt – a kick, taken by a special teams player called the punter, that surrenders possession to the opposing team. This is normally done on fourth down when the offense deems gaining a first down unlikely.

receiver – an offensive player who may legally catch a pass, almost always wide receivers, tight ends, and running backs. Only the two outermost players on either end of the line of scrimmage—even wide receivers who line up distantly from the offensive line—or the four players behind the line of scrimmage (such as running backs, another wide receiver, and the quarterback) are eligible receivers. If an offensive lineman, normally an ineligible receiver, is placed on the outside of the line of scrimmage because of an unusual formation, he is considered eligible but must indicate his eligibility to game officials before the play.

run – a type of offensive play in which the quarterback, after accepting the ball from center, either keeps it and heads upfield or gives the ball to another player, who then attempts to move ahead with the help of blocking teammates.

sack – a play in which the defense tackles the quarterback behind the line of scrimmage on a pass play.

safety – 1) the most uncommon scoring play in football. When an offensive player is tackled in his own end zone, the defensive team is awarded two points and receives the ball via a kick; 2) a defensive secondary position divided into two roles, free safety and strong safety.

snap – the action that begins each play. The center must snap the ball between his legs, usually to the quarterback, who accepts the ball while immediately behind the center or several yards farther back in a formation called the shotgun.

special teams – the personnel that take the field for the punts, kickoffs, and field goals, or a generic term for that part of the game.

tackle – 1) a term for both an offensive and defensive player. The offensive tackles line up on the outside of the line, but inside the tight end, while the defensive tackles protect the interior of their line; 2) the act of forcing a ball carrier to touch the ground with any body part other than the hand or feet. This concludes a play.

tight end – an offensive player who normally lines up on the outside of either offensive tackle. Multiple tight ends are frequently employed on running plays where the offense requires only a modest gain. Roles vary between blocking or running pass routes.

touchdown – scored when the ball breaks the vertical plane of the goal line. Worth six points and the scoring team can add a single additional point by kick or two points by converting from the 2-yard line with an offensive play.

FURTHER READING

Crepeau, Richard. *NFL Football: A History of America's New National Pastime*. Champaign: University of Illinois Press, 2014.

Frisch, Aaron. *Super Bowl Champions: New England Patriots.* Mankato: Creative Company, 2014.

Geoffreys, Clayton. *Rob Gronkowski: The Inspiring Story of One of Football's Greatest Tight Ends.* North Charleston: CreateSpace Independent Publishing Platform, 2016.

Gronkowski, Gordon. *Growing Up Gronk: A Family's Story of Raising Champions.* Boston: Houghton Mifflin Harcourt, 2013.

Gronkowski, Rob and Jason Rosenhaus. *It's Good to Be Gronk*. New York City: Simon & Shuster, 2015.

McKay, Andrew. *Rob Gronkowski: The Inspirational Story Behind One of Football's Greatest Tight Ends*. Morrisville: Lulu Press, Inc., 2015.

Price, Christopher. *The Complete Illustrated History New England Patriots.* Minneapolis: MVP Books, 2013.

Strunak, Mickey. *The History of NFL Expansion Teams Since 1961.* Frederick: PublishAmerica, 2013.

Wilner, Barry and Ken Rappoport. *On the Clock: The Story of the NFL Draft.* Lanham: Taylor Trade Publishing, 2015.

INTERNET RESOURCES

http://bleacherreport.com/nfl
The official website for Bleacher Report Sport's NFL reports on each of the thirty-two teams.

https://www.cbssports.com/nfl/teams/page/NE/new-england-patriots
The web page for the New England Patriots provided by CBSSports.com, providing latest news and information, player profiles, scheduling, and standings.

www.espn.com/
The official website of ESPN sports network.

http://www.footballdb.com/teams/nfl/new-england-patriots/history
The Football Database, a reputable news source, New England Patriots web page providing historical rosters, results, statistics, and draft information.

www.nfl.com/
The official website of the National Football League.

www.pro-football-reference.com/
The football specific resource provided by Sports Reference LLC for current and historical statistics of players, teams, scores, and leaders in the NFL, AFL, and AAFC.

http://www.patriots.com/
The official website for the New England Patriots football club, including history, player information, statistics, and news.

https://sports.yahoo.com/nfl/
The official website of Yahoo! Sports NFL coverage, providing news, statistics, and important information about the league and the thirty-two teams.

INDEX

CHAPTER 1

Jeffrey Beal | Wikipedia Commons

© Jerry Coli | Dreamstime

© Ragarwal123 | Dreamstime

CHAPTER 2

Wellslogan | Wikipedia Commons

© Andrei Tselichtchev | Dreamstime

© Melinda Dove | Dreamstime

Reeseflynn | Wikipedia Commons

Jscarreiro | Wikipedia Commons

Marianne O'Leary | Wikipedia Commons

CHAPTER 3

Andrew Campbell | Wikipedia Commons

© Jerry Coli | Dreamstime

© Scott Anderson | Dreamstime

© Jerry Coli | Dreamstime

CHAPTER 4

© Starstock | Dreamstime

© Eric Broder Van Dyke | Dreamstime

© Steven Cukrov | Dreamstime

© Jerry Coli | Dreamstime

© Jerry Coli | Dreamstime

© Dwong19 | Dreamstime

© Andrei Tselichtchev | Dreamstime

CHAPTER 5

© Starstock | Dreamstime

© Sbukley | Dreamstime

© Mira Agron | Dreamstime

© Christian Delbert | Dreamstime

© Jerry Coli | Dreamstime

© Jerry Coli | Dreamstime

Boston Public Schools | Flickr

EDUCATIONAL VIDEO LINKS

CHAPTER 1

pg. 10: http://x-qr.net/1HoU

pg. 11: http://x-qr.net/1Fwa

pg. 12: http://x-qr.net/1H8Q

pg. 13: http://x-qr.net/1EfJ

pg. 14: http://x-qr.net/1Eii

pg. 15: http://x-qr.net/1E62

pg. 16: http://x-qr.net/1Cr8

pg. 17: http://x-qr.net/1F5v

CHAPTER 2

pg. 27: http://x-qr.net/1DZf

CHAPTER 3

pg. 42: http://x-qr.net/1DuT

CHAPTER 4

pg. 54: http://x-qr.net/1Gf3

pg. 56: http://x-qr.net/1Dcc

CHAPTER 5

pg. 65: http://x-qr.net/1EtD

ABOUT THE AUTHOR

Joe L. Morgan is a father, author, and an avid sports fan. He enjoys every type of professional sport, including NFL, NBA, MLB, and European club soccer. He enjoyed a brief career as a punter and a defensive back at the NCAA Division III level, and now spends much of his time watching and writing about the sports he loves.